EXTREME COLORING

Amazing World

BARRON'S

Get set to take your coloring skills to another level by testing your concentration, color sense, and hand-eye coordination in the challenging world of extreme coloring!

Extreme coloring offers a great opportunity to extend your artistic flair and stretch your creative powers. These intricate pictures have been created especially for those who enjoy immersing themselves in this fast-growing adult pastime. With hundreds of divided sections in each picture, you can be as adventurous as you dare!

The outlines in this book will take you on a whirlwind ride around some of the most famous and most beautiful sights of the world. There are thrilling cityscapes, inspiring landscapes, iconic buildings, ancient and modern feats of engineering, and natural wonders. From the magnificence of Egypt's Pyramids of Giza to the beauty of America's Grand Canyon, and from the wonder of the Taj Mahal to the majesty of Mount Everest, you can create your own works of art with just a few colored pencils, watercolors, pastels, or inks.

There's no right or wrong – you don't even have to stay within the lines – and you can make the images as realistic or as surreal as you like. If you want to replicate the subtle tones of a Tuscan hill town or the vivid colors of the jungle, then go ahead, but you do also have the chance to create a neon-bright New York skyline, a sci-fi blue Houses of Parliament, or a kaleidoscopic Eiffel Tower. So pack your pens and take a flight of fancy to your dream destination. You don't need tickets or a passport, just some colors and a free-wheeling imagination. Have a fantastic trip!

TOKYO, JAPAN

Tokyo, the world's most populated city, is a buzzing metropolis whose skyline is dominated by more than 40 immense skyscrapers. Most distinctive of these is the 50-story Cocoon Tower, with its white aluminium and dark blue windows that criss-cross their way to the top. The city's unique contemporary architecture is illuminated by spectacular colored neon lights and overlooked by the colossal, snow-capped Mount Fuji.

VENICE, ITALY

Known as the most romantic city in the world, Venice
is built on 117 islands, formed by 177 canals, and connected
by 409 bridges. Its elegant decay makes it spectacular in
every season and in every shade of light. The combination of
the gondolas (traditionally painted black), the buildings in
every shade of brown and yellow, and the dreamy canals
produces a magical and enchanted atmosphere.

RED SQUARE, RUSSIA

Built by Ivan the Terrible in 1560, Saint Basil's Cathedral,
with its fairytale-style towers, dominate all the other
buildings in Moscow's Red Square. The cathedral was
originally all white with golden onion domes, but the
domes are now painted in an array of vibrant, bright
colors. Each spire is decorated in a duo of vivid colors
to contrast with the terracotta of the building itself.

MANAROLA, CINQUE TERRE, ITALY

Manarola Harbor may be petite, but it has beauty aplenty.
In this, the second smallest of the famous Cinque Terre towns
in Liguria, Italy, small boats rest on the main street leading
down to the water. Above the tiny harbor, a jumble of tall,
pastel-colored houses are wedged into the cliff-side,
forming a beautiful vertical mosaic overlooking the sea.

WINDMILLS, THE NETHERLANDS

It's springtime in Holland, where the blooming tulips
produce a vivid palette of reds, yellows, pinks, and purples.
This kaleidoscope of color forms a unique backdrop to the
Dutch landscape of wide vistas, distant horizons, glittering
canals, and floating clouds. And, overlooking it all, is the
majestic windmill (there are more than a thousand
of them in the Netherlands, some still in use).

BANGKOK FLOATING MARKET, THAILAND

You can almost smell the mouth-watering scents and hear
the lively chatter on these bustling, floating markets in
Bangkok. The farmers in their traditional blue shirts and
bamboo hats sit on thin, wooden sampans, displaying their
bowls of bananas, rose apples, coconuts, exotic vegetables,
and piles of spices. This confusion of color contrasts
with the murky brown waters of the canal.

EIFFEL TOWER, PARIS, FRANCE

Completed on March 31st, 1889, the Eiffel Tower symbolizes
Paris. For 41 years, the nearly 1,000 ft. tower was the
world's tallest man-made structure and, since opening,
has welcomed almost 250 million visitors. This district
of the French capital has a long association with
innovation – the first manned hydrogen balloon flight
was launched from here just over a hundred years earlier.

GRAND CANYON, USA

More than 270 miles long, up to 18 miles wide and a mile deep, the sheer size of the Grand Canyon in northern Arizona is awe-inspiring, but so too are the vivid colors and shades of the layers of rock. Overall, the Grand Canyon is red, but different minerals in the rocks give the strata distinctive and subtle shades of red, yellow, and green.

HOOVER DAM, USA

In the Black Canyon, 30 miles from Las Vegas, stand the awesome Hoover Dam and the Mike O'Callaghan-Pat Tillman Memorial Bridge. Both of these man-made marvels stand more than 700 feet above the Colorado River. The dam was completed in 1936, while its dazzling companion bridge – the highest concrete-arch bridge in the world – was opened in 2010.

MACHU PICCHU, PERU

One of the most intriguing destinations on the planet,
Machu Picchu (which means "old mountain" in
the Quechua language) is a 550-year-old Incan-built
citadel, nestled on a small hilltop between two forest-clad
Andean peaks in Peru. Rediscovered in 1911, this vast lost
city of the Incas is often shrouded in mist, enhancing the
atmosphere and mystery of these wondrous ruins.

HOUSES, MENTON, FRANCE

Situated on the French Riviera, just along the Franco-Italian border, the village of Menton in Provence is a delight. It's full of beautifully restored old buildings, with a cascade of painted houses – in ochre, red, pink, yellow, and other vibrant colors – spilling down the hillside to the sea. It undoubtedly lives up to its nickname of "The Pearl of France."

COLOSSEUM, ROME, ITALY

Measuring approximately 615 by 510 feet, the massive
stone amphitheater known as the Colosseum was the
largest amphitheater in the Roman world, seating more
than 50,000 spectators. It was commissioned around
70-72 CE by Emperor Vespasian as a gift to the people
of Rome, and for 400 years it hosted gladiatorial combats,
hunts, wild animal fights, and even mock naval engagements.

GOLDEN GATE BRIDGE, SAN FRANCISCO, USA

The Golden Gate Bridge is regarded as one of the seven wonders of the modern world. This immense suspension bridge spans the mile-wide, three-mile channel between San Francisco Bay and the Pacific Ocean. Instantly recognizable by its "international orange" color, it is the most photographed and quite possibly the most beautiful bridge in the world.

GREAT WALL OF CHINA, CHINA

It may be a myth that it can be seen from outer space, but the
Great Wall of China, built more than 2,000 years ago, is still
one of the world's greatest monuments. At an average height
of 25 feet, the wall spans an amazing 13,000 miles as it cuts
through vast and diverse landscapes, from rugged mountainous
terrain to swaying cornfields and green river valleys.

PETRA, JORDAN

Located amid rugged desert canyons and mountains in what
is now the southwestern corner of Jordan, Petra is one of the
world's most famous archaeological sites. Half-built, half-carved
into vibrant red, white, pink, and sandstone cliff faces,
possibly as early as the third century BCE, this towering
structure was "lost" to the Western world for hundreds
of years until its rediscovery in the early 1800s.

LEANING TOWER OF PISA, ITALY

The Leaning Tower of Pisa is one of the great icons of Europe. The tower's famous lean of 5.5 degrees was caused by soft ground on one side, which became apparent before it was even completed in 1310. Made of gleaming white and pastel marble, it has a diameter of 52 feet at the base and would stand 180 feet high – if it were straight.

POTALA PALACE, LHASA, TIBET

Built in the seventh century CE in the Tibetan capital Lhasa, the Potala Palace is the residence of the Dalai Lama. Perched on a 12,000 ft. cliff, this magnificent 13-story building is the world's highest palace. It consists of the breathtaking upper central Red Palace, with its crimson stone and gold leaf canopies, which is surrounded by the outer White Palaces, with their starkly contrasting black outlined windows.

BOATS ON A BEACH, THAILAND

It may seem like another world, but idyllic Thai islands
like this one can be found not too far from the noisy crowds
of Phuket. Here, under beautiful blue skies, mountainous
cliffs overlook forested coastlines, as traditional long-tail
boats bring the occasional visitor to desolate coves
and empty beaches of impossibly white sand.

THE SPHYNX AND GREAT PYRAMIDS, EGYPT

The Sphinx, an enigmatic 242 ft. long limestone monument
with the face of a human and the body of a lion, stands watch
over the pyramids of Giza. Behind it, the Great Pyramid,
one of the ancient Seven Wonders of the World, stands
450 ft. high and was constructed using more than two million
limestone blocks, each weighing an average of 2.5 tons.

TAJ MAHAL, INDIA

An immense mausoleum made of white marble, built in Agra
between 1631 and 1648, the Taj Mahal is the jewel of India.
Its magnificent architectural symmetry and elegant domes
are enhanced by an inlaid design of flowers and calligraphy
using precious gems, while arches cast endless shadows.
Outside, the flawless mirror pool and its lush green
surround provide a perfect frame for the monument.

HOUSES OF PARLIAMENT, LONDON, UK

The Palace of Westminster, better known today as the Houses of Parliament, was built on the site of a medieval palace, which may have been a Roman Temple dedicated to Apollo. Today, it is the site of the House of Commons and the House of Lords, as well as Westminster Hall, the Jewel Tower, and the Elizabeth Tower, which houses the famous clock and its bell, Big Ben.

AMUSEMENT PARK, USA

Around the world, people flock to amusement parks to be
strapped in a seat, thrust along at great speeds, twisted
around and around, or dangled in a swinging car suspended
high above the ground. Modern day roller coasters exceed
100 miles per hour and flip you 360 degrees up to ten times,
while the largest ferris wheels reach over 300 feet.

MANOROLA, CINQUE TERRE, ITALY

The Cinque Terre is a string of centuries-old seaside villages
– Monterosso al Mare, Vernazza, Corniglia, Manarola, and
Riomaggiore – on the scenic but rugged Italian Riviera coastline.
Each of the five towns is built into the cliffs overlooking the sea.
Their multi-colored houses cling to steep terraces while
fishing boats fill the shores of the tiny beaches below.

IPANEMA BEACH, RIO DE JANEIRO, BRAZIL

The bossa nova hit "Girl from Ipanema" put Ipanema Beach in
Rio de Janeiro on the map as a place of sun and sand,
as well as the tanned and lovely. Once in the spotlight, the
resort blossomed, with sun worshippers taking over the
beautiful stretch of sand which runs down from the jagged hills,
while elegant modern buildings filled the nearby streets.

THE STRIP, LAS VEGAS, USA

The Strip is where the action is in Las Vegas: a four-mile neon-lit, palm tree-lined dreamland of casinos, entertainment venues, and hotels. The opulent architecture and décor of the Strip's casinos have made the pedestrian walkways a major attraction, as tourists marvel at the dramatic buildings, including a half-scale replica of the Eiffel Tower.

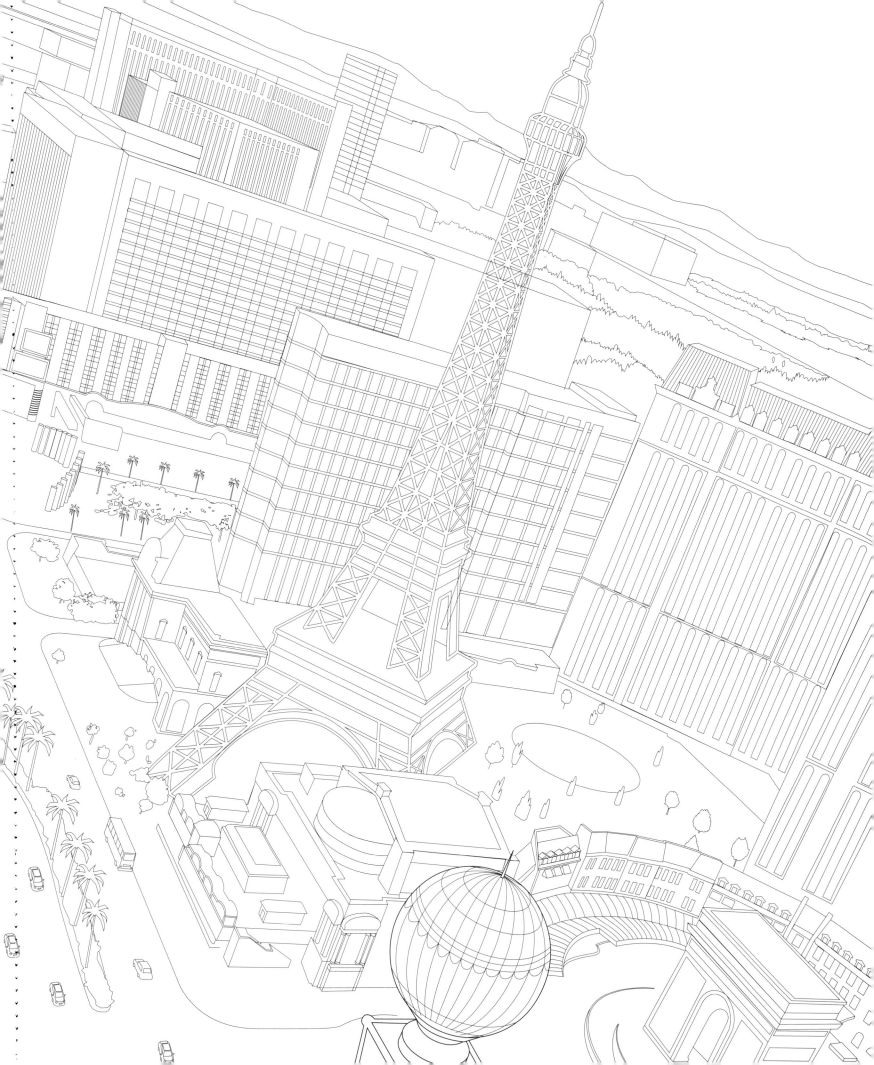

BOSTON, MASSACHUSETTS, USA

One of America's oldest continuously occupied cities,
Boston has some of the most historic buildings in the country.
Once a stagnant pool of water behind the Public Garden,
the neighborhood of Back Bay is most famous for its rows
of three- and four-story brownstone houses, which are
considered to be some of the best preserved examples
of nineteenth-century urban design.

PIAZZA NAVONA, ROME, ITALY

Rome's Piazza Navona, built on the former Stadium of Domitian and constructed by Emperor Domitian in 86 CE, is famous for its three fountains. The view from the north side of the square is dominated by the Neptune fountain, with the obelisk of the central Fountain of the Four Rivers also visible by the Baroque church of Sant'Agnese in Agone.

NYHAVN, COPENHAGEN, DENMARK

Nyhavn, meaning "New Harbor," is a seventeenth-century
waterfront district in the Danish capital, Copenhagen.
Once a tough neighborhood, it is now a popular tourist
spot. Visitors flock to see the waterfront streets and
the brightly colored seventeenth- and early eighteenth-century
townhouses, including the former home of writer Hans
Christian Anderson, as well as a range of beautifully
restored historic boats that lie moored along the dockside.

CENTRAL PARK, NEW YORK, USA

America's greatest park, Central Park in New York City
has over 80 fountains, monuments, sculptures, bridges,
and arches, but many of its 25 million visitors a year use
its great open spaces to look at the busy metropolis
from which they have escaped. It offers some fabulous
views of the architectural delights of Manhattan.

AMSTERDAM, THE NETHERLANDS

Amsterdam, capital of the Netherlands, is defined by
its canals. The city has more than 100 miles of these
tranquil waterways. Dug in the seventeenth century
during the Dutch Golden Age, they form concentric rings
around the city. Many of Amsterdam's canal-side
houses, distinguished by their striking geometric
gables and dual entrances, were built at the same time.

MANHATTAN BRIDGE, NEW YORK, USA

This much-loved suspension bridge, which crosses the East River and connects lower Manhattan with Brooklyn, was designed by famed architect Leon Moisseiff. In the twentieth century, the bridge became an icon of architecture and America, with most suspension bridges that followed it heavily influenced by its innovative design. The bridge's total length is 6,855 ft (2,089 m) and it was the last of the three bridges built across the East River, after the Brooklyn and the Williamsburg bridges.

MUSEUM OF ARTS AND TRADITIONS, SEVILLE, SPAIN

The impressive Museum of Arts and Traditions in Seville
celebrates the traditional crafts of Spain. The building,
known as the Mudéjar Pavilion, was designed by Aníbal
González in a Neomudejar style for the 1929 Spanish-American
Exhibition. González employed aspects of the classic Mudejar,
or Moorish, architecture of the thirteenth to fifteenth centuries,
particularly the use of brick, tiles, and horseshoe arches.

HAVANA, CUBA

Cuba's checkered history has left an indelible mark on
Havana's cityscape. Hundreds of years of Spanish rule saw
houses built in a grand colonial style, but years of poverty have
seen them reduced to faded grandeur. Meanwhile, thousands
of American cars were brought into Cuba before a US ban
in 1962. Ever since, the Cubans have found ways to
keep their prized American cars on the road.

BARRIER REEF, BELIZE

The Belize Barrier Reef is the largest barrier reef in the
Northern and Western Hemisphere, spanning 185 miles of
Belize's turquoise waters. Listed as a World Heritage Site by
UNESCO in 1996, the barrier reef is home to a maze of colorful
reefs made up of hundreds of species of coral, as well as
over 500 species of fish and other marine life.

ANGKOR, CAMBODIA

In the Angkor area of Cambodia, there are more than a thousand temples. One of the most remote – and captivating – is the 12th-century Ta Som temple. Many years of neglect have resulted in a large tree growing out of the east gate, and the photogenic qualities of nature merging with the ornate architecture have made Ta Som an essential destination for camera-wielding tourists.

GUANAJUATO, MEXICO

Guanajuato, in the mountains of central Mexico, was
once a silver mining boomtown, providing 30 percent of
the world's silver. This resulted in a mass of colonial-era
architecture that shot up around the mines. These houses
now cram together on the hills of the city in every
imaginable color; pink houses nestling next to yellow,
and blue buildings standing next to red neighbors.

EVISA MOUNTAIN, CORSICA, FRANCE

Evisa is a spectacular mountain resort, high in the
mountains of Corsica. It is a popular destination for walkers
who come to enjoy the stunning landscapes for which it is
renowned. The village is framed by jagged mountain peaks,
chestnut groves, pine forests, and red granite cliffs;
its bright orange roofs standing out against azure skies.

ST. MARK'S SQUARE, VENICE, ITALY

St. Mark's Square in Venice has long been celebrated by
artists and scholars for its beauty and harmony, while
Napoleon described it as the "most beautiful parlor in the
world." On three sides, the square is lined by stately arcades
of public buildings, but the fourth side is the Basilica
Cattedrale Patriarcale di San Marco, a collection of
domes and arches, with a soaring bell tower.

PARK GÜELL, BARCELONA

One of the most famous sights in Barcelona, the
enchanting Park Güell features wild stone structures,
distinctive buildings, and fantastically colorful tiling,
all designed by the radical architect, Antoni Gaudí.

CAPRI, ITALY

Capri is one of the most picturesque locations in Europe,
celebrated by everyone from Homer to Beyoncé, and
this charming seaside port of Marina Grande is many
people's first view of the island. The bluest of seas
gives way to a small square and steep terraced slopes
of shiny white houses, flower-filled balconies and brightly-
colored walls and canopies, often picked out in "Pompeiian red."

PANAMA CANAL, PANAMA

Opened in 1914, the 50-mile Panama Canal provides a vital
connection from the Atlantic to the Pacific Ocean. The canal,
which uses a system of locks to lift ships 85 feet above sea
level, can accommodate massive ships carrying up to
65,000 tons of cargo. Today, around 14,000 ships use
the canal every year, paying around $1.8 billion in tolls.

STREET, PROVENCE, FRANCE

The winding cobbled streets of Provence reveal sun-drenched
stone houses, adorned with a profusion of beautiful flowers.
Every house seems to feature a multitude of pots and window
boxes, filled to bursting with red poppies, white peonies,
yellow honeysuckle, clusters of hyacinth and,
of course, aromatic Provencal lavender.

NEUSCHWANSTEIN CASTLE, BAVARIA, GERMANY

King Ludwig II ordered the construction of Neuschwanstein
Castle in Bavaria, Germany, between 1869 and 1886, in honor
of the composer Richard Wagner. Built on a rugged cliff
against a scenic mountain backdrop, it has no military or
strategic purpose – it was designed to look like a
fairytale castle and would later become the inspiration
for the castle in the Magic Kingdom at Disneyland.

COTTAGE GARDEN, ENGLAND

The cottage garden originated – and is still at its best – in
England. It conjures up pictures of lazy summer days,
bumblebees, butterflies, and every color of garden flower.
Pots of lavender and geraniums surround pathways of poppies,
cornflowers, and delphiniums, while roses, clematis, and
wisteria provide a natural mural of color on the cottage walls.

JUNKANOO FESTIVAL, NASSAU, BAHAMAS

In the city streets of Nassau in the Bahamas, the cacophony of cowbells, drums, and whistles, and the sight of gyrating crowds can mean only one thing – the Junkanoo Festival. This is the island's distinctive carnival and participants spend all year creating their unique costumes of crêpe paper glued to fabric, cardboard, or wood, each competing to be the most elaborate and colorful.

TRESCO ABBEY GARDENS, ISLES OF SCILLY

The world-famous, subtropical Tresco Abbey Gardens are in the Isles of Scilly. Thanks to long summers and mild winters, this extraordinary place is home to more than 20,000 species of plants from 80 countries, ranging from Brazil to New Zealand and Burma to South Africa. Among them are towering palm trees, giant bright-red flame trees, the great blue spires of Echium, and drifts of shocking-pink Pelargonium.

FLORAL DISPLAY, ITALIAN VILLAGE

We go to an Italian village, a million miles away from the
car horns and motorbikes of the city, where the façade of a
modest cottage simply oozes timeless, rustic charm. From the
window boxes come the sweet fragrances of basil, oregano, and
rosemary. Tomato vines climb around the window frame, while
armfuls of cheerful, colorful flowers fill every space available.

First edition for North America published in 2016 by Barron's Educational Series, Inc.

© Copyright 2015 by Carlton Publishing Group.

No part of this publication may be reproduced or distributed in any form or by any means without the written permission of the copyright owner.

All inquiries should be addressed to:
Barron's Educational Series, Inc.
250 Wireless Boulevard,
Hauppauge, New York 11788
www.barronseduc.com

ISBN: 978-1-4380-0835-6

Manufactured by: Marquis, Louiseville, Canada

Printed in Canada

9 8 7 6 5 4 3

For best results, colored pencils are recommended.

Picture credits: Shutterstock.com and Thinkstock.com